# SIMPLIFICATION

How to be heard and seen in times of information overflow

Benedikt M.
Hugenschmidt

StrateKey

First published in Switzerland in 2019 by StrateKey

Copyright © B. M. Hugenschmidt 2019

The moral right of the author has been asserted.

All rights reserved.

No part of this publication may be reproduced, stored in a retrieval system, or transmitted, in any form or by any means, without the prior permission in writing from the publisher, nor be otherwise circulated and without a similar condition including this condition being imposed on the subsequent purchaser.

All graphics within this publication are the work of the author.

ISBN 978-1-689-11275-8

StrateKey GmbH
Birkenstrasse 14
4304 Giebenach/BL
Switzerland, CH

www.stratekey.com

# Contents

| | |
|---|---|
| Introduction | 5 |
| Why Simplification? | 8 |
| The Process of Simplification | 14 |
| Simplification not Trivialization! | 22 |
| Visualization | 29 |
| Facilitators (Accumulation, Uniqueness and Context) | 35 |
|     Accumulation | 35 |
|     Uniqueness | 37 |
|     Context | 39 |
| Hearing; Get Feedback from Others | 42 |
| The Model of Simplification | 47 |
| Simplification in Use | 52 |
|     In Politics | 52 |
|     In Economics and Business Administration | 61 |
|     In Strategy | 66 |
|     In Media | 72 |
| Elevator Pitch vs. Simplification | 76 |
| Fails in Simplification – the Negative Use | 79 |
| When to use Simplification and when not? | 85 |
| Closing the Loop | 90 |
| Collection of Take Away | 95 |
| Acknowledgements | 98 |
| Works Cited | 99 |

# Introduction

Why writing a booklet on "Simplification"? Is it not a contradiction writing an entire essay on this topic? As the author of this book, I think, "No, it is not. It is about time writing on a subject that is taking so much space in our everyday lives." The background pushing me to write this book, are my observations in clients advisory as well as the way communication takes place in politics, science, and economics.

On one hand, I witness facts being trivialized enormously and on the other hand, I see actualities made over-complicated up to a ridiculous level. Actually, this is applied in the way the communicator wants the topic to be perceived by the receiver. As a recent example, let us take the debates and discussions on Brexit taking place in 2018 and 19. The supporters of a (even hard) Brexit claim three major reasons for it; first – Britain will then be re-enabled to act on its own and independently, second – they can stop sending money to Brussels/the European Union and third, workers from the EU will decline, so they will no longer take away the jobs from British laborers. The Remainers, who want to stay in the EU, design the Brexit as an incredible complex, almost impossible to solve Hercules task, which cannot be achieved due to the interdigitating between Britain and the EU – according to them, this is true in terms of logistics, law, politics, and many other fields. Even in the subtopics of the Brexit, the same form of dispute continues. Brexiteers insist that the political situation with the "backstop-arrangement" for the Republic of Ireland and Northern-Ireland would prevent a final exit of Great Britain forever, whereas their opponents suggest new (complex) arrangements and addendums to be negotiated with the EU. In a nutshell, as an independent and neutral observer, the whole debate appears like an ancient Greek drama. I could continue with examples from this topic, but this would add no additional insights.

If you now have a closer look at the topic and oversimplify the different positions, you will summarize the Brexit position as "good for Britain and it only has advantages" and the Remainers position as "bad for Britain and it only has disadvantages". We all now (even the representatives of the two positions) none of the statements is entirely true; there are advantages and disadvantages in every way forward.

Additionally, this example shows one of the problems of Simplification; as soon as it is pushed too far, it turns from "condensed truth" to blunt assertion ignoring important facts and topics. Imagine the referendum on the Brexit would have only taken part with the two slogans „Brexit is good for Britain", and „Brexit is bad for Britain". Most probably, the major part of the voters would have asked „Why?"

The "art of Simplification" is to condense a subject, product, offer, etc. without eliminating the most important attributes of the core. If you take the images of the cover, you may realize that both images show a sailboat – and exactly this is the core-message. Although the sketch is very "raw", it is recognizable as the same object as on the photograph. Imagine now, the "artist" of the sketch would have left the sail. Then it still would be a boat, but by the missing of one core-attribute (the sail), the "message" of the photograph and the sketch would no longer be the same.

Even though the topic of Simplification is often consequently applied in the external communication of companies towards their clients and between individuals in social networks, much to our surprise it is almost as often skipped in the communication within the same companies or – as an example - in families. Why does this happen and what would change if Simplification would be used consequently in every area of our lives?

# Why Simplification?

Today's world quite often is perceived as complex and complicated. This is especially true for people in the western world, although I have heard these statements as well from people originating from East Asia. Without having made a profound analysis of this phenomenon, I am still convinced the world of today is not much more complex than it was for people living 200 years ago. What changed indeed are the speed and the volume of the available information.

It was only 50 years ago when in various countries no private television- or radio-broadcasting was allowed. E-mail as we know it today simply did not exist and social networks or channels like YouTube were not even imagined by the most innovative people on earth. All information came delayed and via the broadcasting-companies owned or led largely by the government or - as newspapers – with a clear focus on profit. Furthermore, all the news had been filtered and prepared by the editors – this was done mainly because of the limited formats and time being available as well in newspapers as in broadcasting formats. Nowadays, this has changed radically! The major part of individuals in the western world does have the possibility to share an information, opinion, or incident with the rest of the world almost simultaneously at any time he or she wants to.

It obviously is a fundamental strength of mankind to adapt quickly to new situations and so to fit in e.g. changed environmental conditions. This is mostly achieved by using tools and other aids like additional clothes in colder regions of the planet. However, in its very core, humankind does not adapt that fast and such a change needs much more time. Still, typically for our kind we took over the new technological tools fast, and share now images of our food-plates, parties and more with the entire world and send short messages back and forth. Surprisingly, very few of us ever realize that not only they are sending information somewhere, but the entire rest of us do it as well. This initiates the problem of how do we deal with all the information we are receiving in these days. For most people this problem is unsolved, and we are not (yet) capable to process such a constant amount of information inflow. Consequently, the most common way to treat the overflow is "ignoring it".

This is the point where "Simplification" steps in – we are only able to get the attention of our targeted receivers when we simplify it in a way that he or she is able to get the core message with a single glance. To be clear, with the gained attention the message is not yet fully processed in our brains, but at least we get an entry-door to enable a further processing of what we want to be received.

This concept is neither new nor surprising. It is used in marketing and advertising already for decades. As an example, you may take the AIDA principle (AIDA stands for attention, interest, desire, action) which was already described more than 120 years ago in 1898(!). This principle as well starts with the attention of a customer, which has to be achieved first. In our times where we have a certain amount of information-stimulus-saturation, getting the attention is even more crucial. There is the old saying "an image says more than a thousand words" and so it is apparent why platforms like Snapchat or Instagram are booming. A central element of these networks is the picture, trying to catch the interest of the viewers. It explains as well the phenomenon of internet-memes spreading fast and massive on the net with a high response and reproduction rate.

The topic is known from TV ads as well; additionally they frequently add their learning of "sex sells". Let us take the example of a men's shower gel starting with the camera view of a woman in a white T-shirt jogging in the rain; where is exactly the link to the product?

Evidently, the same effect of getting attention is achieved when shocking the receiver of a message. As an example, some of you may remember the ad-poster of a garment-label showing a bloodstained t-shirt and camouflage pants with bullets holes from a killed solder. What is the addressed reaction? Shock!

I intentionally took older examples of ads to illustrate that the topic of getting attention and simplify it to one image, is as old as we are able to put something into a picture. Again, what really changed is mainly the density of information; this conclusively leads to more difficult conditions in getting somebody's attention.

With the rise of social media, the topic of "getting attention" now has widened from a "pure company issue for products and services" towards individuals wanting to praise themselves, their actions, or interests. Selfies increasingly are made from more "extreme" positions and a food plate in a restaurant will be re-draped before being shared as an image. There are many more examples, which can be seen on the web every day. In the end, the goal of all this remains the same – generating the attention of friends, acquaintances, and family-members with a situation reduced to one single image. As soon as I do have the attention, I may transport my message as well. For the sake of clarity, I will not cover the messages of selfies, food-images or similar in this book, but look on the methods needed to get as much awareness as possible without crossing red lines of ethics or morality.

The obvious need for getting attention is widely spread and the – to be expected – increase of information flow will force us steadily to not only getting the attention from a receiver, but as well to transport a message in the same instant to him. This is where "Simplification" uses a methodical approach ensuring the receiver's attention and the message transfer at the same time.

The above used examples have been based on images, since this is the current dominant form for Simplification. Obviously, the topic is not limited to pictures. Company- and product-slogans in the external communication use the same approach and have – if they are done properly – the same effect. Examples? Take "Volkswagen – Das Auto" (this slogan was indeed used in German in the Anglo-Saxon countries as well), "Nike – Just Do It" and "Red Bull gives you wiiings". These three examples transport far more than the simple text-message. They generate attention and trigger associations at the receiver's side. This again addresses the topic of pictures. Quite often associations come in the form of a picture within our minds. Who did not see the VW logo in his or her mind when he read Volkswagen, who did not see the "Swoosh" of Nike before his or her inner eyes, and who does not think of the Red Bull logo of the company or the silver-blue can? Our brain stores information quite often in the form of images, these images can be activated by a simple text message. Consequently, we do have our take away here that,

- a Simplification should always go along with a catchy image (real or in the mind of the receiver)!

At this point, let us do a small self-experiment; please watch yourself and especially try to observe your mouth. As soon as you are ready, imagine the logo of a global fast-food restaurant chain with its golden curved "M"...

What have you been experiencing? Depending on your internal attitude (e.g. if you are vegan or not) you either frowned and now have a dry oral cavity or – if you like this form of food – you slightly smiled and now you may have an appetite for a burger or fries. This obviously is as well influenced by the time elapsed since you last ate something.

Even those body-reactions arose from an excellent form of "Simplification" – it triggered associations of tastes, values, services, goods and experiences and made us reacting towards it – irrespective if we wanted to or not...

In summary, we conclude that we are "exposed" to how our brain works. It largely operates with images, having them stored and associated with additional information. This is useful to force an action, desire and – for us most important – interest in something.

Images can as well be forced in the mind of the receiver by words (e.g. "Wow"), slogans, and entire sentences. Consequently, it is in our desire to catch the interest of an on-viewer with either a real picture or an image generated in his or her mind. As soon as we achieve this, we are standing out of the masses of information-inflows and have a real opportunity to transport our information to the receiver.

# The Process of Simplification

The process of Simplification has five steps (CATCH):

1. Identification of the CORE of the central message

2. Identification of the major ATTRIBUTES of the core

3. Definition of the slogan and the visual TRIGGERS (please note, the visual message can as well be triggered in the head of the receiver)

4. Define the FACILITATORS for the Simplification (Accumulation, Uniqueness, and Context)

5. Test it with a short HEARING

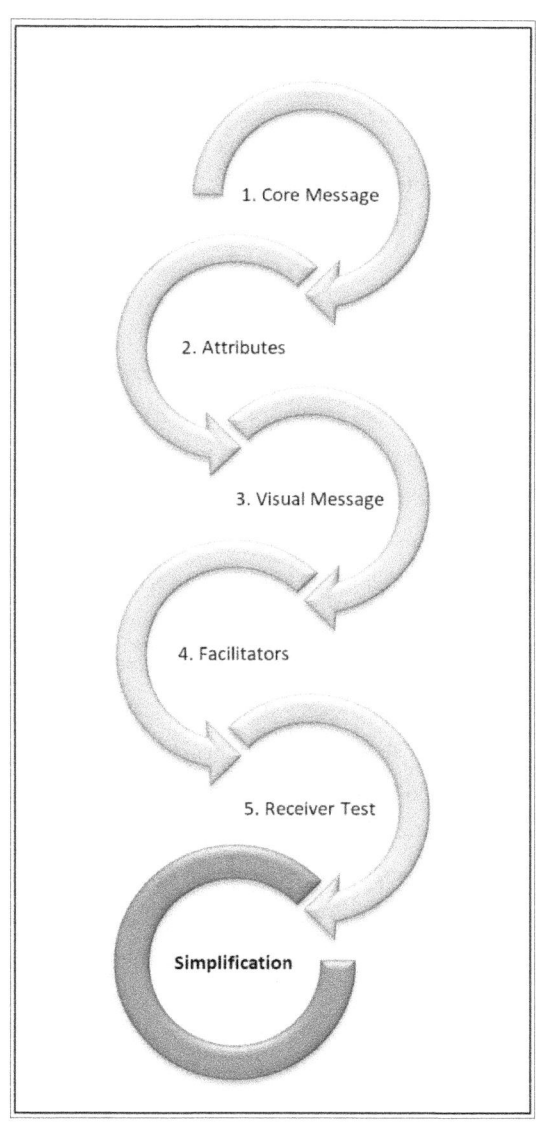

I will deepen the single steps later on. For now it is important, you do understand that this approach is used intuitively by individuals or organizations quite frequently – although on a non-deliberate level.

Additionally, parts of the business like marketing and advertising, use this approach quite frequently already by now. Surprisingly enough, the process of Simplification rarely leaves these departments and stays in its "natural habitat" with the creatives.

In my core activity – which is „strategy execution" – I frequently observe that this process is skipped almost regularly. It became standard in the past years that midsized and large corporates built up so called „strategy teams". One can have different opinions if this is useful or not, but this is out of focus for the time being. The central topic is the self-understanding of these teams. In general, these strategy-teams see their task in the development of a corporate- or business-strategy including the strategy-design and -analysis. As soon as this is accomplished, they transfer the results to an execution-unit (usually the responsible department). From my experience, this often leads to a dilution of the work made by the strategy team. What they typically are transferring is a set of documents and presentations, containing all relevant findings, analysis data, and proposals for the execution. They rarely transfer as well the emotions linked with these documentation to the execution team.

Consequently, the receiving team is indifferent toward the strategy, and it is exactly there where the failure of strategy execution starts.

Obviously, if you are working with such a strategy team, you must have a standardized approach on how to transfer the designed strategy to the receivers. In addition, even if the strategy was developed by the business responsible themselves, it must be transferred to their sub-leaders and teams.

What we see most often is this transfer in the form of a documentation-set. Unfortunately, this excludes almost certainly any kind of emotion and inspiration linked with the work done. At our company, we perseveringly use what we call the "Hugi's Intermediary Step". This has as well the advantage of a structured approach; and – apart from other benefits – it additionally forces the participants to use Simplification. At the beginning of a transfer, we always use the mission, vision, values and the analyzed and designed strategy. As soon as the responsible of the strategy team starts to transfer the information to the execution team, he is forced to formulate the "critical success factors (CSF)". This is – in the notation of Simplification – a message. If it is done properly, it is already a core message with attributes, explaining what CSFs are identified (core-message) and why these CSFs are relevant (attributes). If the preparation was not made accurately, the responsible of the strategy team will face numerous questions from the execution team, forcing him to sharpen the CSF until it finally becomes a core-message with attributes. The same repeats itself with every single step in our transfer model.

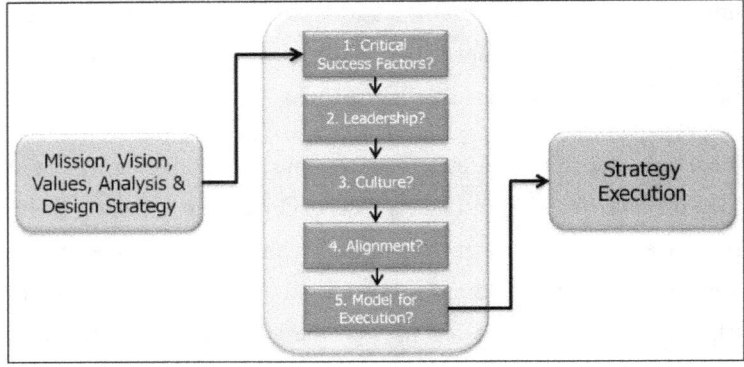

Strategy execution additionally has another strong link to Simplification. Frankly, the vision and the mission are nothing else but Simplifications where the vision is forcing the "what (to achieve)" and the mission the "how (to achieve)". The values define the (ethical) borders in which a company or business operates and the strategy itself, represents the plan. If the vision is blurred or weak, the following parts will not (emotionally) connect and questions will arise. So in consequence, nailing down a vision means producing a short but understandable picture in the head of your listener. It comes without saying that a vision, which consists of more than five short sentences, will dilute the picture in the head of your audience and never ever produce any (positive) emotions, usually the attention of your listeners are then drifting away…

This is exactly where my analyzing "Simplification" in more detail started.

Imagine me, sitting as a consultant in a board meeting of a financial institution where the head of strategy and his team are explaining the new corporate-strategy. The CEO welcomed the board members before and announced the final strategy design. The strategy team already went through several rounds with the same board and refined their proposal with every circuit. My job was to help the company implementing the strategy on the corporate as well as on the department level. Now the "head of strategy" started his "lecture"; he was summarizing the analysis, highlighted the main findings, mapped the market and competition... at least this is what was planned. It took less than three minutes when I saw the first department-head was taking out his "Blackberry" checking his mails (I assume), after five minutes the entire audience, including the CEO was scribbling, using cellphones, etc. while the "head of strategy" was showing slides and his team was sitting upright, keen to answer upcoming questions. Now it is not adequate for me as a consultant to snub clients, so I shortly checked with the CEO and – after a confirmation – I started to ask questions.

What was my first question and who did I address?

Well, it was neither the CEO nor "the head of strategy" – I intentionally took the CFO and asked him "What is the new vision of your company?" I have to mention here I have never met a board member of a larger company who is not bright and fast thinking! The CFO replied and gave me a bullet list of 17 (!) topics representing the new vision. Now, as a consultant, you are already moving on thin ice, asking such questions to your customer; so telling them that this list is not useful is no real option. On the other hand, the topic and I now had the full attention back again.

I asked a randomly picked member of the strategy team, to paint a picture of the strategy on the whiteboard. I received a quite puzzled look and the team-member started to write a line. I insisted I wanted a picture of the strategy and not a written bullet list and this poor person simply asked "How? I cannot do this." Since I did not want to put anyone in the crossfire I replied, "I can't, neither – who in this room can draw it?" Nobody had a full picture in mind and so we started a short brainstorming putting the parts together. Some of them were easy like "global" represented with a globe and "becoming number one" with a podium, others like "cost leadership" were more difficult (in the end we put a dollar sign behind some prison bars). After about an hour we had the core statements visualized and the vision was no longer a bullet list with 17 items, but a picture with five subjects (later they added two more), that everybody agreed on and understood.

When I returned a few days later, I was welcomed by some lower level functions with "See the painter arrives" and "Hello image guy!" Out of pure curiosity, I asked if they could tell me how the picture would look like and they described the picture and the corresponding vision from their heart and without hesitation. In the CEO's office, a flipchart with the vision was installed (now looking much more stylish and professional than what we had drawn in the meeting room) and I have seen self-made copies of it in many notebooks or pinned sketches of it on walls afterwards.

For the implementation of the strategy, this helped since every planned action or service could then be mapped in the vision and led to a better understanding of what to do and why to do it (in a certain way). Actually, all was connected and transparent and therefore better accepted at all levels of the company.

What we did was nothing else but designing a Simplification of the vision, putting it in a form, everybody would remember and be able to reproduce it. With this, we laid the foundation for the strategy-execution, ensuring every member of the company had a common ground to start from when being told what the new strategy was.

## Simplification not Trivialization!

This chapter covers especially the topics of the core message and – to prevent misunderstandings and indifference – how important its attributes are.

A common, quite often made, mistake when using Simplification is to trivialize. This means to drill down a message so much it loses its arguments and consequently its value. An example I already have shown is claiming only "something is good/bad" (e.g. Brexit is bad). If we act like this, we change from Simplification to "claiming" or we are defining a thesis. Now an inherent part of every thesis is that you have to try to prove or revoke it – which usually is a time-consuming and laborious process, meaning it is exactly the contrary of a Simplification. If you are skipping these efforts, then it is really just a claim.

Is claiming badly? I would say no, not per se. In the past (up to some smaller part until today), claiming was an established method in advertising. My favorite one is "XYZ washes whiter!" in a commercial for a laundry detergent. It certainly called for the interest of the receiver. Now, if the ad had stopped after the statement, it would not have had the same effect as it did, when there was a short story where a housewife compared her bed linen drying in the sun with the ones of a neighbor. It was evidently that one set was "whiter" and they even topped it with the statement, "the sun reveals it!" The entire TV ad took roughly 30 seconds.

At this point, I have to open a short window that supports "Simplification". In July 1941 the first TV ad (for a wristwatch), was broadcasted in the United States – it lasted only 5 seconds. This was because filming was expensive and nobody knew how people would react to such a new thing. 15 years later TV ads usually had durations of 60 seconds; the first TV ad in Germany (washing powder) for example took 55 seconds. As a rule of thumb, you may summarize it like that; in the fifties, the average duration was 60 seconds, in the seventies, it was cut half down to 30 seconds nowadays it is about 15 seconds but the share of the ads with 5 or 6 seconds increases dramatically. The reasons for this phenomenon are quite well known and still very much disputed. In 2015, a study[1] of Microsoft Canada was released stating, that our average attention span lasts only 8 seconds. If this value is exactly true or not, is out of focus. What matters is the fact that the attention span is short and if you are not succeeding in getting the attention within this short time-frame, you simply are wasting your (expensive) ad time.

This brings us back to Simplification and the reason why this is so crucial for everyone. Our first focus is on how to prevent trivialization when simplifying messages. Where is the difference when I claim?

- "We're all going to die!"

- "We're all going to die one day!"

---

[1] MICROSOFT, *Attention Spans, Spring 2015,* Retrieved July 30, 2019.

- "We're all going to die tomorrow!"

- "We're all going to die tomorrow because a meteor will strike earth then!"

We all know, bullet one and two are (at least until today) true. We usually do not think about it too much and when we e.g. meet someone in the street holding up a sign-plate with this statement, we look at it, shrug, and pass on without really considering it too much.

If the same happens with a sign plate and the statement of the third bullet, we look at it, shrug our shoulders again and probably think this person is crazy or in some kind of weird sect and pass on. Maybe some of us will ask him why he thinks so.

Same constellation, but with the message of the last bullet; we look at the sign and then? Some of us will do exactly the same as described before, some of us will ask the guy why he thinks so and some of us will check the web or news if this is really predicted.

Obviously, this also depends on the context. If we see the person with the sign (even if it is the last version) every day, at the latest on the third day, we will not take any notice any more from him. If we have not seen this person ever before, the impact of the messages is as described above. And now imagine one day you see not only one guy with the sign and the fourth message, but 15 of them on your way to work, wouldn't you be slightly irritated or even getting nervous?

I think this example shows "nicely" how Simplification works, and how the difference to trivialization looks like. Additionally, three new components are added, called "facilitators";

- accumulation,
- uniqueness and
- context.

As it is in advertising, it is in Simplification. If you miss the right situation to place your message, it will likely be overlooked or overheard. We will have a closer look at these three facilitator-elements in the next chapter.

To check whether your message is simplified but not yet trivialized, just ask yourself or even better someone else "what are the main elements (core message & attributes) of this message?" The answer then should be (to stay with our example); we will die tomorrow (**core**) and due to a meteor strike (**attribute**). It is quite the same as it is in a newspaper; you do have the headline and the subtitle giving more details. A question at this point, what would you write as the headline if you were the editor of a newspaper; "We are all dying tomorrow" or "Meteor strike will hit earth tomorrow"? I think it will strongly depend on the newspaper's general policy and the targeted reader segment, nevertheless, both of these headlines would likely address the attention of people. One has more information than the other does – so people interested in information will likely choose the newspaper with the second headline.

Imagine when you played Pictionary; if the searched term was "a sailboat" you would likely first have drawn ⛵, then ⛵ and finally ⛵. Although I do not claim to be a great artist, I am convinced after the first step of the sketch already a large percentage of people would shout out "a boat." However, if we limit the number to answer to just one single possibility, probably everybody would still wait to see what else is coming. After the second step, many hands would already be hovering above the buzzer and certainly, after the third step everybody would be convinced to know the answer. This shows exactly the difference between trivialization and Simplification. Everybody probably agrees that the final sketch of the "sailboat" is a very simplified version of the reality – still it is recognizable as a sailboat because it consists of a core message (the hull) and attributes (the mast/pole and the sail). Leaving one of these three aside dilutes the message e.g. leaving the mast/pole away might force the imagination that in the end it will be a cradle or even a baby carriage (just the wheels are "still" missing ).

Another – from my point of view – questionable Simplification is part of a strategy statement of a global acting wealth managing financial institution. They claim, "*We want to become the number one wealth manager in Asia.*" First, this is no strategy statement at all; it is certainly much closer to a vision than to a strategy since it does not answer "how" this shall be achieved. Second, even for a vision in my opinion, it is too vague. Do not get me wrong, I am not saying the company does not have a designed and well-elaborated strategy, but the message is reduced to the core and the attributes are unknown. What if the company would have claimed: *"we want to become the number one wealth manager in Asia for "ultra-high net worth individuals (UHNWI)" using best digital services in the region"*? It is somehow better, but leaves still some questions open:

- Asia – starting in Turkey ends with the eastern borders of Russia and China? Really?

- UHNWI – who is included there? Who is not?

- Using best digital services? What does that mean exactly?

I certainly would address these questions to the managers in charge if I was an employee or investor and I bet I would get quite a long answer. I guess some of the addressed persons did not ask and thought "pretty much the same as with the bank A, B and C" which in the end means the bank lost the keen interest of this analyst, investor, or employee. What if the financial institution would have stated: *"we want to become the number one wealth manager in (e.g.) China and India for the top 1% of wealthy individuals granting them personal and digital 24/7 advice, information and transaction services."* The statement is certainly not yet perfect, but it surely addresses the core (#1 in China & India) and its attributes, which catches more of the interest of the addressed stakeholders. Trying to put such an abstract topic into a picture is certainly complex. Still it could be achieved with the flags of the countries, a scheduler, and pictograms of humans and electronic devices.

I hope I did illustrate in the chapter why it is essential to use always the core-message and its attributes to simplify a message and why otherwise it is no longer a Simplification but a trivialization.

I ask you to train this topic and enhance your skills by doing it every day in five cases you are addressed and in three cases where you are the sender of a message. This can as well take place during a lunch with colleagues, in a meeting, etc. Each time ask yourself what is the core-message and what the attributes are.

Take away from this chapter is:

- Avoid bluntly claims (do not trivialize your message)
- Check elements (always must have a core and at least one attribute)!
- Train the topic in day-to-day situations as a sender, but as well as a receiver of a message

# Visualization

"A picture is worth a thousand words" – this saying does not only exist in English, but in the same or similar forms as well in other languages. From my experience, this wide spread of it is an indication there is truth in it. Now, everybody can check this by taking any noun that describes something concrete, think of it and then answer whether he/she had a corresponding image in his/her mind. As an example, you may take "house", "tree", "tiger" and so on.

For Simplification, this means using pictures is essential. In general, there are two possibilities using them. The first one is, as shown above, generating a picture in the mind of the receiver(s). The second one, as well quite obvious, is using a real picture supporting the message.

Let us first have a look of the process of designing a picture in the mind of the receivers. To grant best possible effects, you should consider some simple rules of thumb.

First, you should use words describing a concrete thing, a substantive! Try to imagine abstract words like power, air, or mind. You most probably have difficulties to imagine that as a picture. Maybe you see a pictogram or a photograph you have once seen (e.g. a brain with the word mind), but as you see yourself, you are already using a placeholder and consequently the original word is replaced. Now let us do the same thing with words describing a concrete thing, imagine; a car, a cell phone or an elephant. Most of us will now have seen these objects with our "inner eyes", it is not necessary to use a placeholder for them. Consequently, the message is much less diluted than when we use abstract expressions. Still, there is always an exception and for the nouns, this is words with a strong emotional connect like love, hatred, sadness and similar. If those emotion-linked words work as good as objects or even better is disputed, nevertheless, it is a possibility I did not want to withhold from you.

Next thing when wanting to paint in the mind of your receivers is using the right verb. It is especially useful to be as precise as possible with it. As an example, we illustrate it with "an old dog is walking down the high-street."

Now this is already imaginable, still we can improve. What about:

- An old dog is strolling down the high-street.

- An old dog is sauntering down the high-street.

- An old dog is dawdling down the high-street.

- An old dog is running down the high-street.

These examples should only illustrate how you can vary the general term in a more precise form. If you try to imagine this old dog, you probably see the differences in his movement. An additional effect of being precise with the verbs is that it makes reading more interesting and more "colorful".

In summary, we conclude that when wanting to produce an image in the head of the receiver you should use a concrete object with a form and a precise verb describing the action most accurately.

As it was already mentioned before, you may obviously work with real pictures. This sounds obvious, but it is not. First, good pictures for a Simplification are rare. This mainly because many pictures include far more information than the one we want to transport. This obviously may lead to a diffusion of the message. Second, many pictures are simply exchangeable. I have seen so many duckface-selfies and cannot remember a specific one, same with plates of food or beautiful young people walking on a beach – what is the message exactly and why should I remember it.

Still, there are pictures with an effect! I will never forget the image of a small refugee kid lying drowned at a shore in Greece – and this picture recalls still emotions within me as it did when I saw it the first time. Without any message in this example, but imagine a picture of a red rose in a sand desert like the Sahara. I use this example because it is a quite frequent motive – still if it is done well, then you will remember it because it has a surprising effect by combining desert and a blooming rose.

My suggestion is, you do better use no real picture if it does not support your core message properly. This is the most common error and we are so much used to it. Most often, we do not notice this at all – however, it always leads to a weakening of the message!

Want an example? Remember the last PowerPoint presentation you have seen or given. There is an argument if PowerPoint or equivalents are for good or bad, but in any case, these tools exist and they are heavily used. The problem with PowerPoint is that it is an excellent tool for speakers, lecturers and similar to support their speech by giving them a guide. On the other side having slides with only text on it, usually is boring to death. So we are adding pictures and pictograms "related" to the topic of the single slide, as well as graphs and charts supporting the statements made. The problem with all this is, it dilutes the core message of the entire presentation and usually as well the one of the single slide. Funny or sad enough, only few people complain about it. Obviously there are examples where a graph can support the statement, e.g. if you want to show your market share, using a pie chart is a great way. The same is true if you want to demonstrate your growth and you are showing it with a line chart. Still, even in these cases when the market share or the growth is not significantly, nobody or very few people will remember it by heart after a few minutes. You obviously can trick this with shock or surprise. If – for example – the market share is significantly shrinking and you make a call for action, just use a gravestone with your company logo, and add the date "from and to". Although this might sound dramatic, in some cases it might help as a real call to action. Apparently, I do not recommend using this example – if a CEO uses it, everybody will expect the company to die, else if it is done by a lower level function the chance for this person to achieve a reduced personal standing in the company raises significantly.

As you may have noticed, I just mentioned pictograms. Similar to symbols, pictograms are quite useful when you want to draw the attention to your message, still they rarely support the message itself (there are exceptions, as you will see in an example following later). Conclusively my recommendation is to use them very sparsely. Still, sometimes you do have no other choice but to use such a placeholder (e.g. when the platform/social-network is picture focused like Snapchat). If you do apply them, then it is just for getting the attention of the reader. As a result, you then have to use the core message text to paint a more sustainable picture in the mind of the reader. This then can be very cumbersome since the pictogram remains lingering in the mind of the receiver, preventing any new picture connected to your core message to be mentally generated.

In general we may conclude, that it are always the same rules applying for pictures, symbols, diagrams, and pictograms

A final word regarding the visualization; I need to emphasize to avoid spending too much time with the picture, but to focus on the core-message and the attributes. Quite often, this is done wrongly, and the search for a suitable picture takes more time than the formulation of the message. Always remember; a picture can also be sketched in the mind of the receiver.

Take away from this chapter is:

- Your message should always go with an image. This can either be real or generated in the head of the receiver

- Avoid wrong images – better no image than one that is distorting your message

- Use an interesting language; e.g. not only use "walk" but more precisely and descriptive "stroll"

# Facilitators (Accumulation, Uniqueness and Context)

As mentioned in the previous chapter accumulation, uniqueness and context are important elements in Simplification, too. We call them "facilitators". This is why we will have a closer look at those three by now.

## Accumulation

As already stated before, the mass of information increases significantly for some years now. Along with the increased information inflow, our attention towards a single topic is reduced. For Simplification, this has an impact as well. Although it is obviously possible that you get already the full attention of a receiver of a message at the first time, the possibility for this is limited as long as you do not shock or overwhelm she/he with a picture or text. Consequently – like in advertising – you have to repeat your message to get the required attention of the receiver. Depending on the channel you want to use for the transport of the message – but, unlike in advertising – you do not have to repeat the same commercial repeatedly (which might become annoying).

Imagine the story with the vision statement of the financial institution. The repetition (i.e. accumulation) took place when the sketch was repainted and re-told by participants, when it was so prominently presented in the CEO's office and so on. As it is with products and services it is as well with your message, the best thing that can happen is when people talk about it (in a positive way!). As it has been with our ancestors, word of mouth has always been one of the strongest and most important things to transport information. Imagine you have a talk with somebody who is telling you a simplified message with enthusiasm or joy – his or her body-talk is positive, and the facial expressions reflect this positive perception. You will probably notice it and have already a positive perception, too. Now imagine the same happens again the same day or the day after. You will start to get curious what they are talking of. This was exactly what I experienced with the first iPhone… I had read about it online and in newspapers and actually my first thought was "why should I buy something where I first have to install additional software (which may as well cost), only to be able to use it properly." Obviously, I had not fully understood the entire feature yet; still, I had my Blackberry that was working perfectly fine, so I had no need and urgency to change anything. Some weeks later, this changed. I remember quite well when one of my working colleagues showed us his newly bought iPhone 3. Swiping, touching and telling about all the features and possibilities in such a euphoric way I rarely experienced ever before when talking about a technical device. The same thing happened in the same morning with four (sic!) other colleagues. I still could tell you today the name of everyone as well as how he or she had sparkles in their eyes when showing the device.

Actually, it was not the device or any commercial, which convinced me of the iPhone. It was the reaction of these people and the short time frame – the accumulation of positive reports – showing me their newly bought cellphones that gave me the positive cling to it.

## Uniqueness

An information you have seen before does not stick that much with you as something that is entirely new to you. This simple statement can be underlined by your own experiences; how did you react when you saw your first Tesla, how was your reaction when you first saw a rocket start, have you ever seen a perfect rainbow? The list could be continued. Sadly enough, this works as well with negative experiences; remember what you felt when you first saw a picture of the survivors of a Nazi concentration camp? Do you remember any images you have seen of Vietnam or other wars? Or do you remember the images of a flood, images of a racing car accident, people starving in e.g. Africa?

What did these images do with you then and what do them now, when you see them again? Did you become "numb" towards them? Do you still feel the same as you did, when you saw them for the first time?

Quite for sure not everybody feels less emotional towards these examples; still the larger part of us became "less sensitive" of them with time. Parts of this can be explained with the theory of Kahneman[2] where system one processes experiences already made, while system two is only or mainly active at the first experience.

Briefly, Kahneman explains how our brain works with two different systems. System "One" is fast, automatic, always active, emotional, stereo typifying, and unconscious. System "Two" is slow, exhausting, rarely active, logical, calculating, and conscious. Due to these efforts needed by system "Two", our brain tends to process information in system "One". This works with so-called "priming" – meaning as soon as we hear or see certain trigger-words, we recall already processed information limiting our cognitive efforts mainly to system "One".

Going back to my personal experience with the iPhone I had never seen any similar reaction of so many and different people in context with a "simple" tech device. This made my experience so unique (and probably their experience was unique as well since they had never seen such a "smart" device ever before), and this memory is obviously so strong it lingers more than ten years after still in my mind. Depending on your age, you might have had a similar experience or if you are a decade or younger than I am, you might now think; "what a strange guy, where is the point?" The point is the uniqueness of this experience. I never ever saw such a reaction to any later iPhone or Android device, they have been – in terms of handling and novelty – pure copies of the original, and therefore they have never had the advantage of uniqueness.

---

[2] KAHNEMAN, Daniel. *Thinking, fast and slow*. Macmillan, 2011.

## Context

The third important element in Simplification is context. You may have very important information properly prepared with core and attributes, may have planned the accumulation and guaranteed the uniqueness of it but it still misses to reach the recipients.

As explained in the example with the meteor impacting earth, a single man with the same poster everyday does not start to bother us too much, 15 people with the same message at the same day, never seen before will have more impact.

Putting things in context helps us to process information faster and allows the sender to give the information a bias in the wished direction. There are two important elements when we do this:

First, the message must fit into the situation. Imagine you go and tell about the benefits of meat in a vegetarian restaurant. Although your message certainly will call a response, you most probably will not get through with what you want to be received.

Second, the message should be placed in the right frame. When I use the term frame, then I am referring to the work of Entman, defining framing as: *"To frame is to select some aspects of a perceived reality and make them more salient in communicating text, in such way as to promote a particular problem definition, causal interpretation, moral evaluation, and/or treatment recommendation for the item described."*[3] Currently, this aspect is strongly used in politics and mass media, but it is not limited to those.

As an example we take the word: "winter". You now probably have some ideas and memories triggered in your mind; this can be snow, cold, soup, sledging, Christmas and so on. In fact, these frames can not only trigger pictures, they as well call for sounds, haptics, smells and feelings stored in our brains. Due to this power of frames – represented by words – they are as well useful in triggering certain actions.

A word of warning regarding the frames you are using. Quite often, they are misused to guide the receiver(s) in a very narrow field. I experienced when I had a discussion in on 9/11 in the year 2005 and I asked what had brought the three towers (World Trade Center 1, 2, and 7 (WTC7)) down. The immediate response was that there was no third tower tumbling down and that I was a "conspiracy theorist" (this was the frame). The discussion ended shortly afterwards. I was happy, when the National Institute of Standards and Technology (NIST; an official US agency) released in November 2008 a report trying to explain what brought this building (WTC7) down. I use this example because it nicely shows how a frame can destroy a message (or in this case a discussion).

How often do we hear things like "politically incorrect", "conspiracy theory", "climate (change) denier", "feminist", "gooder" and similar?

---

[3] ENTMAN, Robert: *Framing: Towards a Clarification of a Fractured Paradigm,* 1993.

In the end, the idea of all these labels (or frames) is to put you in a corner and associate you with a specific behavior. This then is either increasing or decreasing the value of what you are telling. Unfortunately, the (negative) use of such frames is increasingly spread nowadays. As an example, you can use Karl Marx. In the German Wikipedia one of its attributes in the introduction is "a protagonist of labor movement", in the English version the term used is "socialist revolutionary" – what does it do with you and your perception towards him when reading the rest of his bio? Depending on your value system and background, one will probably force you to see him in a more positive and the other in a more negative way. You may believe it or not, but the selection of the frame was no coincidence; this is exactly what the writer of the article wanted to do with you. Therefore, my message to you is to be conscious about such frames you are using and try to prevent being too much influenced by them. Be as well aware that it is impossible for you to avoid all these frames in your life. You and almost anybody in this world are exposed to them and they have an influence which perspective we take for a certain topic.

Take away from this chapter is:

- Accumulation, Uniqueness and Context are facilitators for your Simplification

- Use framing in a positive way to help people categorize your Simplification

# Hearing; Get Feedback from Others

Talking about Simplification as well calls for some input from communication sciences. I am referring to the model[4] of Friedemann Schulz von Thun what is called four-sides model, communication square, or four-ears model. In brief, Schulz von Thun states that not only what you are saying, but what the receiver understands matters.

The model states that every massage does have four aspects. As a result, every message can be understood differently by the receiver as it was meant by the sender.

These four aspects are:

- The Factual Information; is simply data and facts

- The Self-Relevance; tells something about the sender (values, motives, emotions, goals, etc.) irrespective if intended or not

- The Relationship; tells how the sender and receiver (or vice-versa) stand to or feel about each other

- The Appeal; finally includes the "request" (instruction, wish, advice)

---

[4] SCHULZ VON THUN, Friedemann: *Miteinander reden: Störungen und Klärungen. Psychologie der zwischenmenschlichen Kommunikation.* 1981.

It is not the target to go into too much detail of this concept. The main thing I want you to understand and consider is the fact, that it is not only what you say that matters, but as well what and how the receiver understands it. Quite often, this is free of any conflict, sometimes it is not. For further details and graphical illustration, we recommend the reader to visit the online presence[5] of Friedemann Schulz von Thun.

As a simple example of a conversation imagine, when a child calls to his/her mother: "Mummy, there is no more milk in the fridge!" Most likely the mother will understand this as an appeal and react (buy, fetch from somewhere else, etc.) accordingly to it.

Now to illustrate the conflict that may arise from such a conversation, we take the same example and change it slightly. It is no longer a kid that is calling, but it is a boyfriend calling his girlfriend (let us say they are both around thirty years old). So he is calling: "Honey, there is no more milk in the fridge!" What happens in the minds of the two actors?

Boyfriend (sender)

Factual Information: *There is no milk in the fridge*

---

[5] SCHULZ VON THUN, Friedemann: *Online Presence of "Schulz von Thun Institut für Kommunikation"*, https://www.schulz-von-thun.de/die-modelle/das-kommunikationsquadrat. Retrieved July 30, 2019.

| | |
|---|---|
| Self-Relevance: | *I want to have milk by now but cannot find it* |
| Relationship: | *You probably have stored the milk somewhere else without telling me* |
| Appeal: | *Tell me where did you store the milk!* |

Girlfriend (receiver)

| | |
|---|---|
| Factual Information: | *There is no more milk in the fridge* |
| Self-Relevance: | *You do want to have milk and it upsets you there is no more milk left* |
| Relationship: | *You think I have forgotten to buy milk.* |
| Appeal: | *I should go and buy some milk for him!* |

The answer of the girlfriend will be: "If you want milk, then go and buy it yourself."

Quite obviously, the single elements of these thoughts might be different in the end – depending on the situation and the mood of the participants – however, this could lead easily to an argument between them due to the different understanding of the message.

Generally, Simplification bears a significant risk to be understood differently than it was meant. The main reason for this is the fact that the message quite often is an appeal in itself. Remember our example, with "We are all going to die…!" What is the appeal of it? Prepare yourself, say goodbye to your beloved ones, do penance, etc.? Even when we do not know what exactly the appeal of the sender was, we can easily imagine that every receiver including you and I might have a different understanding what is called for. This is as well one fact, why the attributes of the message are so important, they usually reduce the simple appeal and give some more insight on the factual level.

For Simplification, this means we must not only consider what we want to say, but as well how it is (how it could be) understood by the receiver. This can easily be done with a grid as the one shown in the example before. Repeatedly done so you do not need the grid anymore and it becomes a reflex to consider the receiver's position.

Additionally and very useful is what in Simplification is called a "hearing". The goal of it is getting the feedback of one or more persons who are similar to the intended target receivers. This does not have to take place in a very formal meeting or similar. If you run such a hearing, just tell the persons you have chosen the context, the intended channel of message transportation and the full Simplification (core message and attributes). Ask them how they perceive the message and what their first impression was – including what they thought was the appeal. If the feedback correlates with your intended goal, then you most probably get the best possible results when launching the Simplification. Furthermore, you have a certain confidence if the intended message goes through. If the feedback deviates strongly from what you intend to transfer, you should re-work your Simplification considering the input you have gotten.

Take away from this chapter is:

- Every message carries/transports facts, an appeal, a self-relevance and a relationship information

- Keep in mind; it is not what you say, but what the receiver understands that counts!

- Consider running a "hearing" to enhance the probability your message is understood, as you would like it.

# The Model of Simplification

Putting now all described elements together, we have the following model. As I stated before, it is important to start from within with the core message.

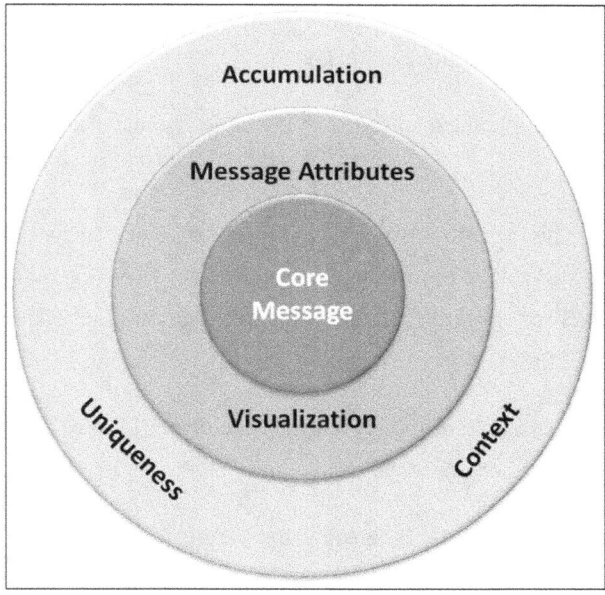

This somewhat very simple model considers all relevant details to get your message heard. The question left open is now, what happens if we do not cover all these six points in our message? Obviously, you can do it, the effect will simply be (much) smaller, and it is questionable if you really achieve what you want.

To check whether you are on the safe side, you can ask yourself now:

1. What is the core message?
2. What are the attributes of the message?
3. What is the visualization of the message – explicit or in the mind?
4. Is there an accumulation of the message?
5. Is the message unique?
6. What is the context in terms of the situation and what frame do I use?

If you are not able to answer all the questions right away, then your message still can be optimized. If you answer one or several question not at all or negative, then your message certainly has some significant flaws.

Taking the example of the person with the poster "We're all going to die!" is a useful example.

1. Core Message:     obviously is answered – we will die
2. Attributes:       no attributes available
3. Visualization:    no visualization
4. Accumulation:     no only this single guy every day again
5. Uniqueness:       from my point of view; No

6. Context: street, by passers do not even look, random message receivers; Frame? Yes – Death (probably not the topic liked most)

The message itself is very clear and straightforward, still apart from the core-message and the frame – which is perceived by most people as negative – all other elements are missing. Consequently, the effect of it fizzles.

Let us take another example. Fancy you write this "message" below and a hacker sets it up that this message pops up repeatedly on mobile phones with a weird sound and/or a strong vibration:

**Warning! Attention! Danger!**

Your device is infected with a dangerous hybrid virus threatening your device as well as you. Immediately run the virus scan and shut down your device afterwards. Wash your hands thoroughly and contact your doctor right afterwards. Do not touch any other thing or person.

Now the vast majority of the readers will smile and say this is ridiculous – and yes for the time being they are absolutely right. But imagine the recipient is not tech-savvy and maybe uses such devices only because he or she is obliged to…

Let us go through the six questions:

| | | | |
|---|---|---|---|
| 1. Core Message: | "you are threatened – be cautious!" | OK |
| 2. Attributes: | biohazard sign, infection of you and device | OK |
| 3. Visualization: | biohazard sign | OK |
| 4. Accumulation: | first by the repeated pop-up and second by the use of a sound and/or vibration | OK |
| 5. Uniqueness: | At least I did not experience anything like this before | OK |
| 6. Context: | Situation: your device is your privacy; recipients will be unprepared | OK |
| | Framing: biohazard sign and headline | OK |

Apart from the question if such a message would be ethically, legally and content wise correct, what would be the reaction of the receiver? Since we are trained and most of us educated in realizing that the biohazard sign means any form of danger (even when we do not know what threat exactly), our body will react automatically. The Hypothalamus forces the release of Adrenaline, Noradrenaline, Cortisol and Cortisone. Sympatico as well as Para Sympatico will be activated and our body prepares for fight or flight.

Consider only for a brief moment this message would be true, then this form of alerting and messaging something to someone would be very useful unless you don't get every second day such a message. This is what Simplification is all about get the attention of somebody or a group, inform them briefly and call for an action.

In the following chapters, we will have a short look at how Simplification is used in some areas of our lives. This list of usage is not conclusive and shows how the topic can be used but – sadly enough – as well abused.

Take away from this chapter is:

- Use the model of Simplification – build your Simplification from inside out.

- Check your Simplification with the six questions before launching it

# Simplification in Use

## In Politics

Words have power, especially when correctly used in Simplification. This is probably one of the reasons why Simplification is used in politics for centuries.

When Sir Winston Churchill in his first speech as UK's prime minister in the House of Commons claimed "... I have nothing to offer but blood, toil, tears and sweat..." then he used Simplification. The speech was something more than 5 minutes long and what we still remember is this sentence. Usually, one would expect that this "offer" would be declined, but due to the circumstances, its brutal honesty and simplicity, it was accepted and guaranteed, the prime minister the loyalty for the upcoming years of war.

What I love about this example is the simplicity of the statement and its clearness. Additionally, it clearly supports all that is written on visualization in the head of the receiver(s). If you ask nowadays, what Sir W. Churchill said, the most common answer would be "blood, sweat, and tears." "Toil" is forgotten most of the time. As mentioned before, it is easy to imagine the three first ones, because they do have a form, generate emotions, and recall a smell – in other words, they are very concrete. In clear contrast "toil" is simply an abstract word that we might replace with a hardworking person in our mind – still then it is a substitute, which is much less remembered.

When it comes to politics, we see clearly how lines between a slogan and a Simplification are blurring. Remember the 2008 campaign of

Barack Obama? His slogan "Yes, we can!" is certainly very well known in many places of the world, however, what does it really say? Change – ok, but what shall change? Let us compare it with another very short slogan, e.g. "Just do it!" Probably most of you immediately recognized this as the slogan of Nike and had the "swoosh" in your mind. Did you have a picture with "Yes, we can!" as well? Second, when thinking about Nike you most probably allocated the attributes by yourself and though of any kind of sports – depending on your personal preferences. What did you think when thinking about Obama? I think we can summarize that some slogans are like "Just do it!" and "Think different!" are Simplifications and others as "Yes, we can!" are not, they are kind of "empty words".

Maybe it is not surprising that this "empty words" topic is raised in the chapter "politics". It is as well possible that "empty words" are used on purpose in politics since it they say nothing and all at the same time. However, it is not the topic of this booklet to analyze how politicians act and communicate. Still from the point of view Simplification, it is rather useful to have a short look at it.

As I have mentioned in the chapter facilitators, politics and media like to work with frames. This is setting the perception of the receiver with a "buzz word" of the intended context. Some recent buzzwords or frames are "immigration", "climate change", or "Islamic fundamentalist". Depending on the party a politician represents he uses a frame to set a topic and then places his/her Simplification within. As an example, take "immigration"; this term is quite neutral in its value and often used within statistics or reports (e.g. from UN). Now politicians more conservative and right usually use the frame

"Foreign Infiltration" (e.g. heavily used by the Brexiteers) which represents in our mind a threat. If the politician is more liberal and left, he/she will most likely use the term "Refugees" which is calling pity and compassion in our mind. Usually, politicians do not have too much time to transport their message and they know as well that – when talking half an hour – few people will remember what they really said, consequently the want to transport one or two simple messages to the audience. This is where they use the Simplification.

When Mr. Trump calls "Make America great again!" whom does he address? What is the frame he is using, what the core-message and what are the attributes of it?

Let us look at it a little bit more systematically:

| | |
|---|---|
| What is the core message? | America can be greater than it is right now and I will make it happen! |
| What are the attributes of the message? | None – D. Trump did not say in his claim how he would do it. However, he did it in his speeches, e.g. import taxes. |
| What is the visualization of the message – explicit or in the mind? | The flag of the USA and a bald eagle |

| | |
|---|---|
| Is there an accumulation of the message? | Absolutely. He used the slogan frequently, had posters, buttons, TV ads, TV reports, social media ads and reports and many more |
| Is the message unique? | Absolutely. He dared to say America (the USA) is no longer, what it has been… |
| What is the context in terms of the situation and what frame do I use? | Context was obviously the US presidential election. |
| | Frames; D. Trump used various frames, one of the best known is certainly the emigration from South America ("We build a wall and let them pay for it"), others have been "China" ("Trade Gap") or "Islamic Terrorism" (Muslim ban but never called so) |

Imagine what would have happened if Donald Trump had called the (planned) wall at the border an "iron fence"? Yet not proven since it did not happen, but it is easily imaginable some people would have established a mental connection to the "iron curtain" we know from the cold war. Most probably, this would have a lesser positive effect, since some people still remember how times have been then and how it was living in fear. Another possibility would have been "steel fence", the problem is steel usually is associated with cold and hard and building somewhere such a fence means you are acting exactly in that way, which in the end is as well less desirable in our value system. So taking the "wall" was not only a pure coincidence. We all know walls and we all have a different understanding of it or a different image in our mind when we think of walls, still it is not per se negative associated and walls can as well protect us – this is exactly the association D. Trump intended to address.

There are as well "funny" examples of Simplification and even funnier is the fact they worked somehow. The "strangest" one was the German election of 2013. Chancellor Angela Merkel was already for some years in charge and her party the CDU placed poster ads with the slogan (translated) "Germany's future in good hands" including a picture with two hands forming a rhombus with the index fingers and the thumbs – the so called "Merkel Raute" (Merkel rhombus). It worked extremely well. Without even showing her name or her picture people associated the add 100% with Angela Merkel and they knew what was meant with the message. Media took up the topic and the ad and reported on it; consequently, the coverage was very high in Germany. Finally, it was – at least in Germany – new and unique. Political ads usually work with a slogan, a promise, and a portrait of the candidate, this was skipped in parts; the portrait was only in the head of the receiver and the slogan as well as the promise was merged into one. It was left up to the receiver to decide what "in good hands" exactly meant.

One of the best-known images in politics is Sir Winston Churchill showing the victory sign – although it was not him who invented the sign – he most probably is still the best-known "user" of it. Showing this V – formed with one hand – transfers the message, "I/we have won!" This sign – and Simplification – is already so well known it is not even necessary to add a text. When used correctly, the receiver(s) know exactly what it means e.g. after an exam "yes went perfect", after a sports match "yes, I have won", after a court trial "yes we won" and so on. I ask the reader to be attentive and realize how often this sign is used in so many different situations.

A last topic to mention for current reasons is Simplification in the area of right-wing populism. It does not matter which western country I chose, it is quite broadly spread and it looks their share is growing. It is certainly out of focus to go into details why this happens, still most people would agree that those parties succeed when addressing the people with their messages – and they use Simplification massively.

As an example, I would like to take an ad used by a political party in Switzerland showing how a black sheep is kicked out of the enclosure by some white sheep. The subject was that foreigners with a criminal record (in Switzerland) should no longer be allowed to stay in Switzerland. Now the political opponents called the ad to be racist because the sheep kicked was black. Sorry to say – and this is no political statement at all – but this is simply not true. The illustration goes back to a saying using the term "the black sheep of the family" for a family member acting differently than it is expected from him/her.

Although I do not agree with the exponents claiming that the ad was racist, they have been right in the perception that this ad addressed as well individuals with open or latent racist opinion. If this was done on purpose or not is out of focus of this booklet. Still, this example shows one of the strengths and problems with Simplification. The method is highly useful to address different groups with one single draw. Therefore, the poster was useful to address xenophobic people as well as such who had the wish that people with a criminal record should not be allowed to stay or even get asylum.

However, why is this additional useful for populist parties? Currently, the so-called political correctness prevents many people from saying what they think because they fear it could be understood differently than it was meant. I do understand people when reading in the news that e.g., a refugee raped a woman and then they do not want this refugee to be sheltered in their country – their background then is not racism but a sense of justice or injustice. Moreover, their rejection then is focused only on the individual that committed the crime. Still if they dare to say that this person should be penalized and afterwards be expelled from the country, nowadays they soon will be "branded" as racist. This may generate frustration. Now, as soon as there is a party telling and supporting what they think or feel, some of them see the opportunity to get a voice that is heard without being exposed to the individual risk to be called a racist.

Populists use this insecurity of persons to say what they think, and work with images and texts, which are still within the boundaries of the law (maybe at its borders) addressing a topic the receiver has the same or similar opinion. By reducing it to a core-message and an image, they rarely cross a line, which would identify them as racist, sexist, xenophobic, homophobic, or anything similar. Now people with the same opinion in this single point tend to vote for this party although they do not agree with the party in its entire program.

I had talks with various people from the Austria, Germany, Switzerland, Great Britain, and the USA and none of them was a racist! Still some of them voted for a populist party, Donald Trump or the Brexit because they said that it/he supported their opinion in a certain point that other parties denied, neglected or did not even consider.

Since it is often used in politics, it would have been a significant gap not writing on this topic when talking about Simplification. Furthermore, it is especially in this area where you can see that a good thing can as well be misused and turned into something bad. You may compare it with Dynamite; when Alfred Nobel invented it, he saw its application in mining and wanted to reduce accidents in this area making loose black powder obsolete. It took the glimpse of an eye when military detected the benefits of Dynamite as well…

Take away from this chapter is:

- Avoid empty words and give your Simplification always its attributes

# In Economics and Business Administration

Writing on Simplification in economics and business administration is somehow difficult. This is not so much, because there are no examples of Simplifications used, but because the topic is ambivalent in its appliances. As mentioned in the beginning, advertising and marketing use this form already for a long time in a very professional manner, and as shown in my example with the strategy, within companies the topic is disregarded at all levels quite frequently. As mentioned as well, the extensive use of PowerPoint or similar presentation software is a problem. Some people think on every slide should be an image, which often leads to bad examples of Simplification, and a neutral observer asks himself if the image or the content of the slide (e.g. the core-message) took the main share of the preparation time.

Having a more structured look at it, we first consider economics. A large part of Simplifications we meet linked to economics refers to statistics and consequently come up with a statistical diagram as the corresponding image. There are other examples as well. If there is anything about trade, quite often a container ship is used as an image, when it is about Bitcoin, its logo (the one with the B and the two vertical strikeouts) is used, if it is something about stock-market quite frequently a trading floor of a bank is shown (irrespective that these trading floors rarely exist anymore) and if it is about mortgages most of the time an image of a house is displayed. From the point of view Simplification, there is only one problem with this form of illustration – it does only support the topic but not at all the core message. So people will remember having read or heard about the topic, but the exact message will soon be forgotten. It is key in Simplification to support the message with the (mental) image and nothing else. The use of such images implies either the sender of the message did not reflect what the core message was or he/she just took such an image habitually.

A harsh contrast to this behavior comes from advertising. While in the past the core message of the advertising was a simple "buy me!", it lately implemented the aspects of attributes telling the customer "buy me, you will get this and this value and have that and that advantage!" As an example, you may take mattresses that recently are pushed more on TV ads. In the past the message was, "buy this mattress and you will have a better sleep!" Nowadays it is "for a better and healthier sleep, buy this mattress online, we will deliver it to you and you may test it for e.g. 90 days. If you are not satisfied, you can return it without cost and you will be refunded." The corresponding image is a mattress in a parcel, easily unpackaged by one person. This is just a random example, chose one product you like and compare the advertising made ten years ago with the current one. You likely will realize that the new form is longer and gives much more detail. However, you may as well have noticed that the form changed from a blunt "appeal" (as explained in the chapter "Hearing") to a form of dialog where elements of factual information ("you may return it"), self-relevance ("we care for you") and an appeal are contained. Put in other words; the message was simplified by adding attributes to the core message and enhancing the picture not showing only a logo or an image of a product (e.g. mattress).

Now this is not only taking part in TV ads, but obviously as well in online marketing and on paper.

The apparent question is now, how to close the gap between the educated use of Simplification in marketing or advertising and other contributors? The simple answer obviously is by applying the steps of Simplification (CATCH). To be fair, we have not looked too much into detail of the posts made by some company representatives on LinkedIn, Snapchat, Twitter, and similar – some of them are excellent in terms of core-message and attributes, others are less. What most of them have in common is the "unlucky" use of pictures – as described in the entry of this chapter – or plain company logos. So in the cases where the message is already simplified, it is suggested to invest more time in finding an equivalent picture! Taking the example of mortgages, why not combining an image of a house and overlay it with a graph showing rising of falling tendencies depending on what the sender wants to tell! For the ones not simplified at all, I simply recommend to apply CATCH.

Still open is the optimization of presentations when using software. Simplification suggest you start the presentation with a big "bang" – putting all you want to tell on the starter slide as a Simplification with core-message, attributes and visualization. After you have done so, usually you have the full attention of your audience. This allows you afterwards to tell your story how the initially presented Simplification shall be achieved. Now, you evidently do not have to paint a new picture on every slide, but simply link it to the already shown Simplification. This does not mean you can paint now boring slides with too much text or number listings – the general rules on how a slide should be prepared remain!

In general, the room for improvement in terms of Simplification in economics as well as in business administration is broad. Admitting that such topics are complex and the interdependencies are numerous sometimes, this should not deter you from using Simplification. If you intend to publish or present some content, you already have a message in mind. Therefore, it is only a short way to Simplification and drilling for the essential core of the message. As soon as you have identified it, it is well-invested time to look for the visualization. Admittedly, things are getting a bit more difficult with images since most of the topics in economics and business administration are abstract. This demands for a visualization with a real image since painting a mental picture is – as illustrated in the chapter "Visualization" – not sustainable enough. As already illustrated and implied in some parts, a good or at least useable approach is the combination of subjects. Meaning you first have to transform the abstract words into something concrete and then to combine them. As a simple example, imagine you want to report on a decline in global GDP. For the topic "global" it is useful to work with a globe; for the decline, working with a line-chart. Now you could use the globe and overlay a semi-transparent chart of the GDP development. This will certainly work somehow, but it is not ground breaking – what about replacing the measure-dots on the chart with small globes? As soon as the dots are recognizable as small globes, you get a better response than when doing it the more conventional way. Apparently, you still have to add other relevant attributes and consider the facilitators; still this is a possible way on how Simplification works. As well as it is in other areas, it is in economics and business administration – use Simplification wisely and rare on topics you really think they are worth it.

Take away from this chapter is:

- In economics and business administration, Simplification has room for improvement. The challenge in this area is to transfer abstract terms into something concrete, making them mind-sticking.

# In Strategy

From my very personal point of view, Simplification should be used far more in strategy. It is essential that everybody within the company understands the strategy and acts accordingly. Considering where strategy comes from – the military – it becomes obvious that understanding what we do and why we do something is important. Imagine a soldier who suddenly starts thinking "well, my order is to approach the opponent headquarter silently and take them by surprise, but I am going to do this differently and just fire as soon as I like." He most probably will ruin the entire plan, and it is likely he will put other comrades in significant danger. Therefore, it is important that the soldier knows what to do, why he/she does it and what the implications are if he/she fails. You may obviously say now, "yes, but this is tactics" and you are right. Nevertheless, what if a platoon commander gets the order to get and hold a bridgehead, and he decides to take instead another place that is easier to defend? The result will always be the same; the plan (strategy) will not work out anymore, and consequences can be fatal. Why do I work with these examples? There are actually two reasons. First – as already mentioned – strategy comes from the military (or at least this is where it is documented for the longest time frame), second in armies all over the world the plan (strategy) has always been visualized – be it with models, plans, maps or reliefs. The idea is and was always the same – get people to understand the entire picture. Now it is as well obvious not every soldier or officer has the entire picture and knows every detail, this would be too dangerous and expose the strategy to be transferred to the opponent. Nevertheless, every soldier understands the reason why he/she is doing what he/she is doing on the macro and the micro level. If you consider D-day on June 6, 1944, I bet every soldier knew exactly they wanted to end the regime of the Nazi in Europe and he knew as well when the boat or the plane landed where he had to go. He probably had no idea of the operation "Overlord" but still he knew why he was doing what he was doing.

Keeping this in mind, we come back to corporate and business strategy. A hierarchy says Vision, Mission, and Strategy/Strategic-Goals. Sorry to say, but it is a pity how few employees on all levels have a clue what the vision and mission is all about, they just get some goals (which hopefully are aligned with the strategy) and are expected to fulfill them. In general, you can put companies in four classes (based on what we have seen):

1. Companies with no strategy or only parts of it (e.g. missing vision)

2. Companies with a vision, mission and strategy not told to the employees

3. Companies with a vision, mission and strategy told to the employees, but fully or in parts forgotten by them

4. Companies with a vision, mission and strategy known by the employees

You might say now it cannot be that a company has no strategy or it is unknown to the employees. Well then go and ask e.g. your hairdresser what the strategy of the company is. It is ok for such companies if they have no strategy and just focus on their core-business done with excellence. If your hairdresser is part of a chain or a franchisee then the situation already changes and he/she should know what the "brand" stands for.

Anyway, for cluster one and two I have frequently heard the explanation that the strategy cannot be told to the employees because it is *confidential*. Sorry to say, but this is pure nonsense in every possible situation! It is completely ok and understandable if not all employees do understand or know every single detail of the strategy, however, it is mission critical they know the bigger meaning (vision) and the part of the strategy relevant for them. If not, you are lucky if they just execute what they have been told and do no further thinking about it. In this case, it is obvious you will exactly get what you have asked for. Any improvement is impossible and if you missed considering one or more things, they will never be addressed or changed.

Obviously, for cluster four in terms of strategy no further action is needed (except you probably want to know why all the employees know the relevant details and how this can be reproduced in the future). Our focus consequently goes to cluster three (and one and two as soon as they realize this "confidentiality thing" is of no use) and we come back to Simplification.

As already mentioned, we have so much inflow of information we are barely able to process it. With Simplification, you have a tool to make things stick in the mind of your staff. So – as already shown in the introduction – why not visualizing your vision, mission, and strategy using Simplification?

Please be aware of that the cognitive limits[6] of all of us are 7 +/- 2 – meaning you can only remember a limited size of information on a topic at a time. The impact for your strategy – you want to be remembered by your employees is – you have to limit them to seven Simplifications maximum, and this already includes some people will not remember all topics. If your vision is already as complex as shown in the example in the introduction, then a step-by-step approach should be applied, meaning you are extending the time you introduce your vision, mission and strategy to your teams. As soon as the vision is understood and the majority knows it by heart, you may continue the same process with the mission and finally with the strategy.

It is important to understand that introducing a strategy by using Simplification is not a one-time task! As pointed out in the facilitators chapter, accumulation is important! So having done, e.g. a presentation on the topic, make sure everybody has a handout with the Simplification to take with him/her, pin the visualization – with the message - at boards, posters and similar so that they constantly have the opportunity to review it.

I have an example showing what does not work and annoys people. A service company placed the sentences of their value system

---

[6] MILLER, GEORGE A.: *The Psychology of Communication: Seven Essays: Review". Journal of Business Communication. 5 (2): 54–55.* 1968.

(without any images) as the screen saver desktop for all employees. After some days, nobody was looking at it anymore, and some people even complained about it.

The effect of this action was quite low. It would have been different if it had been supported by an image and even more important, if the employees could have chosen this screen-saver image by themselves. Quite sure not everybody would have taken it, however some would have and their empty screens with the message and the image would have been seen by others as well e.g. when they left their workspace for meetings or equivalent. The impact would have been better in any way.

Apart from these hangouts, posters and other reminders it is as well important to speak repeatedly about your vision, mission, and strategy and link it to the receiver's day-to-day job. What makes Simplification so useful in this area is the fact that all elements can easily be packed in a core message supported by images as well as they are interconnected making it easy to draw a "file-rouge" from the vision to the strategic goals. Supported with images this increases the memorability of all components significantly and allows telling a clear and aligned story.

Take away from this chapter is:

- Simplification is highly useful to align people to a goal or target

- Do not annoy people with forced confrontation of the simplified Strategy but repeat on a constant level with a link to their daily work

# In Media

I think it is worthwhile to have some short reflections on Simplification in the media. As mentioned before, we are used to Simplification, since we see them frequently in all kinds of ads on various channels. It is suitable to distinguish between classical media like radio, newspaper and TV and new forms of media like social networks of all forms as well as messenger apps.

Although strongly inspired by what I have seen and experienced in social media the topic of Simplification goes far beyond that. One of the kick-starters for the topic has certainly been the so-called tabloid journalism/rag newspaper – showing large and simple headlines and a corresponding picture. Best always worked with topics like gossip, crime, sports, and extreme views on different topics (mainly politics and socials). I think it is easy for you to discover that their concept and Simplification are quite similar. The main difference between them is the fact that with Simplification you want to achieve attention on a topic more serious or at least less lurid.

Considering now more "serious" newspaper, we see they follow the same rules in principle. They as well have to generate attention and interest. Furthermore, they are judged by their readers (and yes, now you must read the paper and not only the headlines) on the quality they deliver. What is amusing about this – although they claim to offer a quality product – they act not so differently than the rag newspaper. As an example, take the first edition of "The Illustrated London News" from May 14, 1842. On the front page of the paper is a drawing of "View of the Conflagration of the City of Hamburgh" and a corresponding article – to be noticed; it was in 1842! Therefore, when it gets to getting attention, the concept is not really new. There are other examples dating much before this example e.g. examples of printed papers with illustration of witch-trials and similar. Although I would not call this journalism, the concept stays the same and it is a form of Simplification.

Let us now have a look at TV. When TV started, it was mainly for news and information, it did not broadcast 24 hours and it was essentially an extension of what people already knew from radio. The short history of the commercials I have already mentioned before. Now, when private TV stations started, the competition grew, and entertainment was quickly expanded and it took a significantly larger part of the programs. Amusing enough, this includes as well programs with gossip and reports on celebrities. Apart from TV ads, which follow the rules of Simplification, the entire program of some of those stations follows the concept of Simplification. This includes news broadcasts and news channels as well. Just have a quick look at one of them and answer yourself which information/news are really relevant and which are more built around some images to get your attention and keep you hanging on? Just a hint, why are news always starting with a preview of the topics they will cover. If they are really convinced people watch the news because they want to be informed, then why is this necessary?

Now, what about the new media? I am primarily talking about social networks, messenger services, and video/picture platforms. When doing so, I must confess that lines between them are blurring more and more. It is not necessary to name the platforms simply because they come and go and I am convinced this process will continue.

The most extreme form I have noticed certainly is "Tinder". In Tinder the message is for all the same "I want a partner" (not really more specific than that) and you simply add a picture of you and maybe some short text – obviously the picture should show you in your best light. Now other users – depending on what you are looking for men or women – see your picture and either swipe left or right (no or yes). If both users swiped "yes" then a connection is established and you may start chatting with each other. You may now say that the attributes are missing. I think the attributes are there present as well, e.g. you can define the search radius and there are several options to increase frequency our image is shown or how you can push your image to be shown to a specific other user. All these options are obviously bound to pricing while the standard service is free of charge. Still, the most important part for the attributes are unquestionable your pictures and maybe your text.

However, back to social media in general, I mentioned before that the different platforms are approaching each other more and more. It does not matter if it is good "old" Facebook or LinkedIn, the number of pictures with shortest messages increase steadily. Independently of the fact that one has the reputation of being more for friends and family whilst the other one more for business. A clever approach is used on YouTube showing Ads before they show you the selected content, the only "downside" of this approach is the user may skip the commercial after five seconds. As a paying customer, you may avoid this, but usually customers on YouTube do not pay for it. Now if you are the one who places an ad in this slot, you want to make sure to transport your entire message to the receiver. Meaning you have two possibilities – either produce a spot, which is maximum five seconds long and transports all the information you want to be received or producing a spot, which will be watched in the entire length, meaning you must catch the consumer's interest within the first five seconds. I guess both approaches will end up in pure Simplification. For the first one you simply keep it short and want the customer to picture it in his mind, for the second one you produce a commercial which first gets the attention and interest of the receiver and then you explain the details after the first five seconds.

Therefore, it is all about getting attention in a vast mass of information. In my very personal opinion, it is unlikely this tendency will change or reduce significantly in a near future and it is possible you will see the five seconds ads first approached on YouTube as well in other channels.

Take away from this chapter is:

- The pressure to get attention and transport your core message at the same time increases steadily irrespective of the channel you choose.

# Elevator Pitch vs. Simplification

Have you ever been confronted with a so-called "Elevator Pitch"? The basic scenario of such a pitch is, you are meeting someone important in an elevator and you have only a very short amount of time (the time you would spend with the other person in the elevator) to explain your idea as well as its core message and value. This method is often used in sales and project work and focuses only on the positive aspects. The main target is to convince the vis-à-vis of an idea and to generate a lead for a follow-up.

The advantage of this method is certainly the simplicity of the method, and – as soon the sender is experienced in the method – the preparation is quite easy and consuming only a minimum of time. Disadvantages are that you focus only on the positive aspects so the message is rarely balanced and the content usually is condensed and strongly basic. As the name says, it is thought to be a pitch and not an entire value proposition or concept. In practice – especially in sales – this is where the most common mistake shows up. As soon as you respond to such a pitch and want to have a follow-up, you frequently are confronted with the fact that in a detailed conversation there is only few more on the positive side; moreover, usually on the downside there suddenly will be a lot of "if" and "but" as well as a bulk of limiting information. Obviously, this in a harsh contrast to what the idea of the pitch initially was meant to be.

Now in general the elevator pitch is a really great and useful tool. However, conversations made "only" in elevator pitches are superficial and somehow annoying. After having heard a certain amount of elevator pitches in one sales meeting, you are usually fed with it and want to elaborate some more details on some of the topics.

Having a closer look at elevator-pitches and Simplification, we see the following differences:

a) Elevator pitches are always made as oral personal statements whilst Simplification is mainly used in offline conversations (still can be used in a direct dialog).

b) In an elevator pitch you must convince with the statement and your personal appearance, in a Simplification the mental or real image is the carrier of the information

c) An elevator pitch always focusses on the strength and advantages of a proposed solution, contrary a Simplification may only transport an information free of valuation

d) An elevator pitch is principally thought like a teaser for a follow up, whereas a Simplification is usually a closed complete statement where generally no further actions are targeted


So much about the differences between these two tools, still there are commonalities as well.

a) Both require a certain amount of preparation and should not be made thoughtlessly but careful.

b) Both aim for the attention of the receiver with a condensed form of information.

c) Both require a very short amount of the time of the receiver to achieve the attention

d) Both lose their effect on the receiver when used to frequent.

So both of them are similar still different. The use of them can be complementary, but neither one nor the other needs each other and they can be used completely independently. In general, they are thought to be used on different channels, targeting a different goal.

Take away from this chapter is:

- Elevator pitches and Simplifications are not the same, but can be used complementarily

- An elevator pitch always needs a follow up; a Simplification is usually a complete and closed action.

# Fails in Simplification – the Negative Use

Simplification is not the answer for every question or problem. When trying to explain a complex topic, it is unwise or – depending on the subject – even unethical to use this approach. As an example, we may take the one I have constructed in the chapter "the model of Simplification" with a hybrid-virus. I know that many people laughing at it and call it to be totally unrealistic which is true. Still, some people could believe it and feel threatened. If I use this scheme to generate an action of the receiver then it is unethical.

Sadly enough, sometimes this works quite well and people are forced or even blackmailed in a similar way, forcing them to spend some money to get rid of the perceived danger or exposure. However, it is a fail because it violates the rules we defined as a society. Without naming any country, company, or product, I can give you some examples.

The one that hit me most in the past was a recommendation for a vaccination. At least in certain countries it is allowed to make commercials for vaccination, and I am completely indifferent to it. Still, this ad was saying, "If you are not vaccinating your kid, then you are responsible for that!" It showed an image of a crippled child in a bed. The poster was placed in a pediatrician's office. Now looking at it from a point of Simplification, it was perfectly made at the right place. Regarding the truth of the message, I cannot make any statement since I have not studied medicine and consequently cannot say anything about it. Still – from the point of the receiver – I see this message as unethical. First in my personal opinion, doctors and pharmaceutical companies do not have the task to scare people, but to give them hope; second, the message is a blunt lie. When I did some research, I discovered that the ratio of kids having this illness lies with 1 to 250'000, furthermore, that the possibility to cure the illness is above 90%. Consequently, this image simply represents a very small probability this really could happen to your child of 0.0000044% or 1:2'250'000. What is not told, is the probability of significant "vaccine damages" that may show up. This probability is reported as 1:2'400'000. Conclusively the risk either suffering from the illness or having a significant problem with the vaccination is almost the same.

Another one was when certain governments decided to oblige producers of cigarettes to print disturbing and disgusting images on the cigarette packs with the message; "Smoking kills!" I guess from the point of view Simplification, this topic was treated quite perfectly, still I have never met a smoker stopping this unhealthy habit because of the images. Furthermore, most of them do not look at the pictures anymore. Moreover, it seems the effect on starters is not as well as large as intended. Statistics show a quite balanced number of smokers over the years, meaning consumers stop smoking are replaced with new ones. I am perfectly convinced smoking is unhealthy and a waste of money, but obviously the desire (addiction) is stronger than any action – including price increases, no-smoking areas, disgusting pictures, etc. – taken against it. Although I am really against any efforts trying to move or motivate people with fear or threats, unfortunately all these efforts and especially the Simplifications on the cigarette packs did not work at all. What I have learned from people is, they did get used to it, and the image has no effect on them anymore. Obviously, this is not an official study or statistics, but my simple and plain observations as well as feedback I have gotten from smokers. Still, I guess we can summarize that the constant "pressure" on the smokers with these images lead to habituation and ignorance of it. Intended effects have been lost.

There are other fails; typically, it is about advertising posters and quite a few examples can be found on the web. For reasons of copyright, we will not show them here. However, just check "Advertising Fails" with your preferred search engine and you will find dozens of examples and pictures where something went wrong. When doing so, you will realize quite fast that most of them failed due to their placement, which in our term means context. One of the funny ones is a banner right in front of a cemetery postulating, "Come and join the fun!" Actually, it means a Christian community but due to its placement, its message is completely distorted. Considering that the examples you find on the web have at least a funny element (and so probably a certain advertising value as well), you may imagine there are dozens of ad placements where there is a "weird" combination with the surrounding, that destroys the entire message. Due to the lacking fun of it, they are simply not shown on the net.

So much for the corporate world, but what about fails in Simplification made by individuals? You may remember I wrote in the beginning of this booklet I will not go into the details of messages of food bloggers and similar. Still, I want to take an example, which is somehow linked to this area. It has been some time, when a footballer posted a short movie about himself where it was shown how he got an impressive steak covered in gold leaf served and how it was filleted. He as well messaged a text saying that there was no better start to a new year than this (actually, the message was slightly longer and added some additional attributes). Now it is quite difficult to decipher the real message he wanted to transfer with this video e.g. "I can afford this", "life is beautiful", "I love meat", "Wow, look what all exists", "I am happy", etc. It is out of my scope to drill really into that. Whatever the message was, it completely missed the target. In short time it developed a shit-storm towards him, saying he could have done better with the money, that he was a boaster and many (worse) things more. I would bet this was not what this footballer had expected when he posted the movie. Let us assume he just wanted to share a happy moment in his life with all his friends and followers. He probably did not even think at this moment that anybody would attack him for this because he simply was happy (this is visible in the video) and wanted to share this. Actually sharing happiness is not too bad, right. Still, it turned out bad for him, and he had a lot of TV, newspaper and social media coverage over this. My point with this story is that he (probably) did not reflect what the message he was sending was and – as stated in the chapter "The Communication Square" – he did not consider how the receivers perceived it.

Having written that, I have to add a personal experience. Last year, a friend of mine stayed in Siberia. He posted a selfie of himself in winter saying, "Hi guys, it's freezing cold here (minus XYZ degrees) but we are in a very good mood." Now most of us sent him a smile or a thumps-up still suddenly somebody came up with a reply: "is this a bearskin you are wearing?" What was happening after this question was a back and forth on the topic bearskin. So, even if my colleague just wanted to give a status on how things went and wanted to greet his family and friends, he was suddenly in the middle of a (little) storm. I think it is somehow a sign of the times that every single word or picture may generate a feedback storm with the labels "political correctness", "social responsibility", "climate change" or anything similar, and there is always somebody feeling offended by something you write or show. Sadly, but if you are active on social media channels you probably have to accept this to a certain degree and it is unlikely you will be able to prevent this over time.

Nevertheless, it is important what you share and how you share it! Imagine my friend and the footballer did not show a picture of what they were doing, but simply wrote e.g. "Everything is well here, although freezing cold!" and "Had an excellent start with a great steak into the new year!" probably nothing would have happened, and the feedback would have been positive in general. However, they added the picture/movie intentionally to underline the message and show what they were up to – and! – to get more attention. Well, they got it.

As I have already written in the chapter Visualization a picture is worth a thousand words. Just remember; it might not be necessarily the words, which you would have chosen to tell your story. For my friend (he actually did not post selfies anymore afterwards) it probably would have been better to write – "it's so cold, even my beard is frozen" – like that he would have had generated a picture in the mind of the receivers and avoided the stressing feedback.


Take away from this chapter is:

- Repeating the message too often may change the effect of attention towards ignorance

- A picture is worth a thousand words – but make absolutely sure the picture tells exactly the story you want to

# When to use Simplification and when not?

Simplification is necessary and useful, but there are obviously limits to it. I would not suggest you to use Simplification in a dialog with another person or in a group due to the very simple fact that Simplification is a tool or method for message sending. In a dialog, it is essential you listen and reply to the topics raised by your counterpart(s).

We always must keep in mind what the basic idea of Simplification is; to transport a message to a receiver and get his attention in an environment where too much information flows towards him or her. One goal is always to stand out of the masses. By its very nature every Simplification needs some time for preparation, although the time needed for preparation reduces itself with practice significantly, it is rarely useful in discussions (both business and private) unless it is not prepared in advance. If you are in the position to introduce or present something new or you are opening a meeting, then Simplification is a great tool. However, if you are a participant and you want to illustrate your point of view, you should avoid any Simplification at all.

Considering it needs a certain amount of time to prepare the Simplification, using it during discussions means that you are either not listening to the reasoning in the discussion or you have been all the points already through before the discussion took place and I wonder why you then take part in it. Definitely, your participation in the conversation is doubtful. Therefore, if another participant understands the concept of Simplification, this is exactly what he will realize and – even worse – think of you.

Additionally, and this is true for any kind of conversation, do not try to simplify each contribution from you. Use Simplification sparsely and wise. The reason for this is obvious, using it all the time leads only to what we want prevent with Simplification. Applying it too frequently results in less attention from peers, subordinates, colleagues, bosses, partners, friends and whosoever, since they get used to the fact that you are communicating like this. Consequently, you do not get the same amount of attention anymore. Now talking in pictures to any listener has indubitable its advantages and always helps to understand what is meant. But sending a message with its attributes every now and then is soon perceived as "preaching" by your receivers. As far as I understand only very few people want to be perceived as preachers and only some people like to listen to preachers all the time.

So much said about how you should not use Simplification, additionally the use of Simplification for scaring people is all the same an idea, which is unwise and likely to backfire eventually; the question remains when to use Simplification best?

As a rule of thumb, it is recommended to apply it when you can close your eyes and visualize it immediately for your own. In a session with other people only use it to open the sequence or – if you are experienced in using it – as a summary at the end. On social media it depends on the frequency you are posting something, if you do it multiple times a day, then a Simplification should only be used once a day, if you are posting not on a daily, but weekly basis you may use it once a week. If you are a rare contributor on social media, you may use Simplification every time you are posting.

When advising our clients, we are using the method strongly in strategy execution and especially for the elements of vision and mission. Frankly said, if you cannot visualize your vision, you may draw it in the bin right away. It is the word vision itself that claims to be a view of the future. You probably think this is trivial and obvious. Although this fact should be unquestionable, you probably would be surprised how few "visions" really can be visualized! They are more a kind of ideology – most of the time too complex – that once was noted on a sheet of paper without having any real value and is not looked afterwards anymore. As already told before, it can be far more than this and become one of the crucial success factors when it comes to strategy execution. This is not so much, because it was pushing the execution forward, but because it is the common ground for the entire involved personnel. For us it became standard, first to ask for the vision and its visualization (that is Simplification) when starting a project with a new client.

A further example of use is when you have to make certain announcements, e.g. in your company, your department or for another group of persons. With Simplification, you make sure everybody has seen the core information and he or she will remember it. For people interested in further details you should make them available "behind" your Simplification, without a need for everybody to read the entire story. In that context, Simplification can be a tool for saving time and resources on the receiver's side. As an example, imagine you have a memorandum announcing a new member of the board in a company with 500 employees. It is certainly important for everyone to understand who is on the board. When using Simplification you may transfer the image of the newly engaged member of the board and add some critical CV dates of this person. For 90% of your employees, this information is sufficient and can be processed within - let us say - 10 seconds. Assuming, the information took 450 x 10 seconds, the result is a 75 minutes processing-time within your company. If you had done this with a one-page flyer including picture, CV and some statements, saying it needs 2 minutes to process it, then the same 450 persons would have invested 900 Minutes. The resulting difference is 13 hours and 45 minutes that are invested in productive work or information collection. Now this example is for a quite simple topic, imagine the amount of time saved, when doing it with a more complex issue like strategy.

Finally yet importantly, Simplification is obviously only one way to communicate on online platforms and social media. The way it is exactly used depends strongly on the specific platform. The communication in Twitter and Snapchat deviates strongly from the communication on Facebook or LinkedIn. When working with Twitter, Snapchat, or equivalent, you simply must use an image, or you will be overlooked. Therefore, the image is an imperative on these platforms. If working with Facebook, LinkedIn or equivalent you could work without an image – still I would recommend it there as well. Remember, in Simplification; the goal is always to use a picture that supports your message to 100% or even tells a part of it.

If this is not possible and the platform asks for a picture (Snapchat, Twitter…), then you should consider not using this platform for the transport of your message or continuing finding a corresponding image. Ignoring this, is likely leading to a dilution and distortion of your message

Take away from this chapter is:

- Although depending on the channel, Simplification can be a great tool to reduce invested time required by the receiver to process information.

# Closing the Loop

When started, the story why we came to Simplification was told. At the end of this booklet, we want to close the loop and explain why strategy execution and its topics are so much related to Simplification.

First, we think it is important to repeat, that a vision statement is nothing else than a Simplification per se. Depending on the receiver's level of involvement and responsibility, it already contains the most important elements. It is a fact that quite a few people and amongst them even some academics think vision and mission statements are obsolete and a strategic plan with a strategy map will do. Without going into too much detail, their position is comprehensible. What we see as vision and mission, sometimes is not worth the paper it is written on, and it was only made because of everybody does have such a set. However, for such cases I understand the reluctance of these people towards the vision and mission. Now if you are involved in strategy execution, you will quite soon realize that a common foundation of all involved people is far more than a simple paper exercise. It is likely the one element helping you to start the implementation or change with aligned and educated people. You will certainly lose less time in re-negotiating the topic all over at each level again because all involved persons know the bigger picture. To be clear on this, it does not mean everybody does fully comply with the strategy! However, even if not 100 percent agreeing with it, they do understand what the overall goal and direction is. This is what had to be said about the value of the vision statement.

Considering the mission statement, it usually consists of three core components:

- The target market,
- the product or services delivered
- the reason why the target clientele should buy the product/service (e.g. USP, cost, quality)

Another way developing a mission statement is answering the questions: Who is our client? What do we deliver? How do we deliver it (for business strategies) or where do we deliver it (for corporate strategies)? Since this is not a book on strategy development, we do not go into details about this topic. There are more differentiations and versions of what a mission statement should consist. However, in general, these two descriptions cover the main elements and serve for the illustration sufficiently. As you may have realized, the definition of a mission statement really "demands" for visualization and Simplification.

Obviously visualizing all these elements – or as well the vision – is not a trivial task, especially when you consider that – to keep the image sticky – concrete nouns work better in memorization than any abstract descriptions. Still the efforts are worth it; imagine starting with the vision as a first core message with an image, then adding the mission elements followed by the strategic goals and finally the action plan. In the end, you do have a single picture with layers and on each one of them one single core message. This is having as well the advantage you may add or remove layers depending on your audience. So if you are talking to the press or the investors you may show only the vision and mission, if you talk with your senior management you add the strategic goals and when the senior management talks to lower levels, it may as well add the action plan. I have to add here that there are many different opinions on how the "strategy pyramid" should look like. Some take the mission before the vision; some add the values as well and do skip another element. For Simplification, it is not crucial which pyramid you are applying – although I must confess visualizing values is a trickier task than e.g. visualizing the vision. However, keep in mind that it is not about visualization but about Simplification. This means the image must support the core-message and not the other way around.

Having mentioned the ongoing discussion if vision, mission, and values are useful in strategy or not it must be mentioned that for the analysis and design the value of the three elements might be disputable. However, when it comes to strategy execution the story looks entirely different. In execution, the (mental) alignment of people is one core element, telling them the details and nitty-gritty stuff is completely useless, unless they have a broader picture of upcoming changes and adjustments.

Considering that about 60 – 90 percent of strategies fail due to non-execution, the discussion should probably go in a different direction. It must be considered on what has to be done to make vision, mission and value statements more relevant! With this booklet, we tried to illustrate how this can be achieved by using Simplification. Furthermore, we have shown how Simplification can be used and applied as well in other areas – irrelevant if you use it as a company or an individual.

Simplification is not the answer to each and every problem in communication or strategy execution. Still, it covers some aspects, which are relevant for us. We experience that temptation is always there to skip the model of Simplification and focus only on visualization. Obviously, we may not recommend this, since the focus on the core message is much more important and grants that your information remains the central element. So stick with the model and build it inside out, first formulate your core-message without any thought of the visualization! Add the attributes and only then consider how you could illustrate it – quite frequently, when you have finished the attributes, an image already pops up in your mind. If this did not happen, try to reformulate it and use concrete nouns describing it. Always remember, the image can always be painted in the mind of your receivers, still if you do not have a picture in mind, how should then a listener develop such a picture?

As a final example serves the speech of former US President John F. Kennedy, held at the Rice University on September 12, 1962. When he announced the US Space Program, he said "*…We choose to go to the Moon! We choose to go to the Moon…We choose to go to the Moon in this decade and do the other things, not because they are easy, but because they are hard…*"[7] This is a perfect example of a

---

[7] KENNEDY, John F.: *Moon Speech – Rice Stadium. NASA.* Retrieved July 30, 2019.

vision without any real image delivered but generating it in every single head of the entire audience.

I am completely aware that not every one of us has the same speakers-skills as John F. Kennedy had. However, this should not prevent you from acting exactly the same way as he did, when it comes to transferring the core message.

Especially nowadays when almost everyone has access to social media with its various different forms, it is possible to make an impact with Simplification; transporting a clear and straightforward core-message, its relevant attributes and a coherent (mental) image.

# Collection of Take Away

- A Simplification should always go along with a catchy image (real or in the mind of the receiver)!

- Follow a process when simplifying, use the "CATCH" approach

- Avoid bluntly claims (do not trivialize your message)

- Check elements (always must have a core and at least one attribute)!

- Train the topic in day-to-day situations as a sender, but as well as a receiver of a message

- Your message should always go with an image. This can either be real or generated in the head of the receiver

- Avoid wrong images – better no image than one that is distorting your message

- Use an interesting language; e.g. not only use "walk" but more precisely and descriptive "stroll"

- Accumulation, Uniqueness and Context are facilitators for your Simplification

- Use framing in a positive way to help people categorize your Simplification

- Every message carries/transports facts, an appeal, a self-relevance and a relationship information

- Keep in mind; it is not what you say, but what the receiver understands that counts!

- Consider running a "hearing" to enhance the probability your message is understood, as you would like it.

- Use the model of Simplification – build your Simplification from inside out.

- Check your Simplification with the six questions before launching it

- Avoid empty words and give your Simplification always its attributes

- In economics and business administration, Simplification has room for improvement. The challenge in this area is to transfer abstract terms into something concrete, making them mind-sticking

- Simplification is highly useful to align people to a goal or target

- Do not annoy people with forced confrontation of the simplified Strategy but repeat on a constant level with a link to their daily work

- The pressure to get attention and transport your core message at the same time increases steadily irrespective of the channel you choose.

- Repeating the message too often may change the effect of attention towards ignorance

- A picture is worth a thousand words – but make absolutely sure the picture tells exactly the story you want to

- Elevator pitches and Simplifications are not the same, but can be used complementarily

- An elevator pitch always needs a follow-up; a Simplification is usually a complete and closed action.

- Although depending on the channel, Simplification can be a great tool to reduce the invested time required by the receiver to process information.

# Acknowledgements

This paper could not have been written without the support and the insight I gained at my customers so I want to thank them first.

Furthermore, I want to thank my company giving me the opportunity, the time, and the infrastructure to achieve this paper.

Special thanks go to Markus Baur and Beat always challenging me to bring my inputs down to the point without skipping the train of thoughts.

Finally yet importantly, very special thanks goes to Shadi, Kian, Nik, Damian and Gisela – it is not easy to cope with someone who is constantly twisting his thoughts back and forth with you in a repeated manner. So thank you especially for your patience, your inputs and for telling me I was an exhausting person when I thought and acted like one.

# Works Cited

[1] *MICROSOFT, Attention Spans, Spring 2015,* Retrieved July 30, 2019.

[2] KAHNEMAN, Daniel. *Thinking, fast and slow.* Macmillan, 2011.

[3] ENTMAN, Robert: *Framing: Towards a Clarification of a Fractured Paradigm,* 1993.

[4] SCHULZ VON THUN, Friedemann: *Miteinander reden: Störungen und Klärungen. Psychologie der zwischenmenschlichen Kommunikation.* 1981.

[5] SCHULZ VON THUN, Friedemann: *Online Presence of "Schulz von Thun Institut für Kommunikation", https://www.schulz-von-thun.de/die-modelle/das-kommunikationsquadrat.* Retrieved July 30, 2019.

[6] MILLER, GEORGE A.: *The Psychology of Communication: Seven Essays: Review". Journal of Business Communication. 5 (2): 54–55.* 1968.

[7] KENNEDY, JOHN F.: *Moon Speech – Rice Stadium. NASA.* Retrieved July 30, 2019.

# The Author

Benedikt M. Hugenschmidt is a former manager in the banking sector. He was responsible for the electronic offering to be developed for bank's clients in the ramp-up phase of the internet. He now manages a consulting company with the focus on strategy execution and acts as lecturer at different business schools covering the topic of the book as well as strategy execution. He holds an MBA.

www.ingramcontent.com/pod-product-compliance
Lightning Source LLC
Chambersburg PA
CBHW070801220526
45466CB00013B/1566